# Ripples

## Engaging with the world in prayer

John Birch

# DEDICATION

For the many who have offered encouragement.

# CONTENTS

# ACKNOWLEDGMENTS

Thanks to the many who follow my daily postings on the Faith and Worship Facebook page, as this is this main source for the contents of this book, and the daily encouragement to take time out at the start of the day and concentrate on nothing more than a single prayer thought. It is an interesting discipline for one whose thoughts are normally very scattered and disorganized!

Many of these prayers were published in an eBook of the same title in 2015, which has now been updated for the printed edition with an additional 100 prayers.

,

# 1 : MAINLY OURSELVES

In the busyness of this day
bring peace,
a moment of tranquillity,
sacred space
to be alone with you
and listen.
In the busyness of this day
dear Lord, bring peace.


Put a song into our hearts -
an uplifting melody,
words to inspire,
a time of worship
at the start of every day.

Bless the strangers
I meet today, Lord;
in café, bakery,
bus stop, car park,
crowded street.
Their lives a mystery,
sorrows, joys, loves
and deep concerns
so well disguised.
But bless them, Lord,
these unknown faces,
make this day
one of encounter,
not only with strangers
but also with you.

The choices we make today
impact not just on our lives
but on others around us
and, as a butterfly flaps its wings,
on the wider world outside.
So today, Lord, in the choices
and decisions we shall make,
help us to think not just of self
but of the wider implications,
and ask ourselves, what would you do?

Guide us, gracious Lord,
as we make our way
through this week,
your feet revealing
safe paths to follow,
your calming voice
giving confidence
to continue, through
unfamiliar, challenging
and often beautiful places.


Speak through my words Lord.
May they bring wisdom,
healing, comfort,
encouragement
and humility.
May they speak out for
justice, freedom,
truthfulness
and equality.
May they be your words, Lord.


Take these hands,
these hearts
and souls,
all we have
and all we are,
as our daily
offering to you.

Bless the week ahead.
May its challenges
not overwhelm us,
circumstances
not discourage us,
and in all things
may we remember
you are with us
in our journeying,
your love our fuel,
your word our guide,
today and always.


Lord, bless our journey
through this coming week.
May the pace be steady,
paths made safe,
no obstacles impede,
and conversations
with fellow travellers
be fruitful and uplifting.
Lord, bless our journey
through this coming week.


Thank you for the gift of this day,
may we accept it gratefully,
unwrap it carefully,
and use it wisely
as you the giver might expect.

Thank you, Lord,
for this new day,
the privilege
of travelling
a little further
in your company.

Bless the day ahead,
and through its joys,
sorrows, frustrations
and difficulties
continue the process
of building and equipping
that is enabling us
to become your touch
of healing and comfort,
and messenger
of encouragement
and blessing, to those
in need of your love.

Bless the work we do,
the words we say,
the love we share
and the grace we show,
on our daily walk
through this beautiful
and precious world.

God of love and light,
be seen and felt within
the simplest gesture -
a welcoming wave,
a greeting, smile,
a helping hand,
a 'Give me five'.
God of love and light,
be seen and felt within
each of our lives today.


God of rising sun
be the warmth that I feel
God of gentle wind
be the air that I breathe
God of refreshing rain
be the cleansing I need
God of sacred space
be the peace that I crave
God of setting sun
be the rest I desire


Take that which we are,
the potter's chosen clay,
and with your hands
create from us
something beautiful today.

Circle us, Lord, with your love,
be the warmth seen in our smile.
Circle us, Lord, with your peace,
be the calm within our hearts.
Circle us, Lord, with your joy,
be the song we choose to sing.
Circle us, Lord, with your arms,
be the life we choose to live.

Be in my rising,
the air I breathe,
rising sun,
gentle breeze,
nourishment.
Be in my traveling,
strangers met,
friendly smile,
heart to heart
questioning.
Be in my resting
the peace I feel,
calming voice,
healing balm,
everything.

Good shepherd
walk with us.
Bread of Life
sustain us.
Living Water
refresh us.
Spirit of God
work in us.
Word of God
speak through us.
Three in One
embrace us.


May this be a day of hope,
of expectation,
and relishing each moment
as a gift from you.
May this be a day of joy,
of breaking free
and loosening the shackles
that are binding us.
May this be a day of peace,
and healing,
knowing our lives are
always in your hand.
May this be a day of love
and blessing,
living as children
of a living God.

God of the journey,
the light
by which we see,
the comfort
when we stumble,
the word
that lifts our hearts,
the footsteps
we shall follow,
be our companion
through this day.

Your kingdom come, Lord
in our hearts and worship;
Your will be done, Lord
in our lives and service.

Grant us, Lord,
listening ears,
eyes that see,
willing hands,
humble hearts,
words that speak,
faith that stands.
Help us, Lord
to be everything
that we should be.

Lord, teach us
to become
imitators of you,
and encourage
those of us
who learn slowly.

Help us to accept with grace
those things we cannot do
and concentrate instead
upon the gifts we have from you.

Thank you
for the privilege
of life,
for the beauty
of life,
for the love
of life,
for the joys
of life,
for the tears
of life,
for the hope
of life.
Thank you.

Creator God,
causing sun to rise and set,
warm these hearts with your sweet love.

Jesus Christ,
living water, word of life,
pour into these thirsty hearts.

Holy Spirit,
divine presence, comforter,
guide these feet to safer paths.

Three in One,
who is unity and peace,
embrace this, your fragile earth.

That your name
might be glorified, lifted high
above the turmoil in this world.

God of wholeness, God of Grace,
to you we bring our thanks and praise.


In this busy world
that we inhabit
grant us space
to rest awhile -
by the still waters
of your peace,
to hear the whisper
of your voice
and feel the warmth
of your breeze
within our souls.
Grant us space
to rest awhile.

To a world that searches
you are a lamp that shines,
to a world that is hungry
you are food that sustains,
to a world that suffers
you are hope of release,
to a world that's broken
you are one who restores,
to a world full of hate
you are love that forgives,
to a world that denies
you are truth that endures.
To you we bring our thanks and praise,
God of wholeness, God of Grace.

Help us forgive
as you forgive,
release the pain
we hold so tight,
open our heart,
let it fly away,
for in doing so
we are set free.

The door is open, Lord.
Come, sit beside me
for a little while,
that I may quietly
rest in your presence
before we step out
together into the world.

Healing Spirit, touch this heart
and open wide its door,
that all might be welcomed in
to share your love and warmth.

Take these hands,
let them touch the world
with love and grace
as if they were your hands.

Tale these feet,
let them walk a world
that's full of need
as if they were your feet.

Take this life,
and use it, Lord, I pray.

Spirit of peace,
flow through my life.
Be in the air I breathe
and the words of my mouth.
Be in the bread I eat
and the work of my hands.
Be in the water I drink
and the life that I give.,
Spirit of peace,
flow through my life.

All I am, and all I have,
I offer, Lord, to you.

I offer you these hands,
that you might use them
in and through my daily work

I offer you these feet,
that you might lead them
to someone who needs my help.

I offer you these shoulders
if you should them
to help lighten another's load.

I offer you this voice
that you might use it
to speak up for those in need.

All I am, and all I have,
I offer, Lord, to you.

In the solitude
and grandeur
of a mountain range,
or the restlessness
and clutter
of a city street,
you can be found,
for you are
everywhere,
if we can but see.

Speak
through the world
in which we live.
Speak
through thunder
and driving rain.
Speak
through the calm
of setting sun.
Speak
through ocean
and crashing waves.
Speak
through hillside
and glorious views.
Speak
through whispers
and starlit skies.
Speak
through the smile
of new-born child.
Speak

Yours are the footsteps I follow,
and in which I plant my own.
Yours are the hands I hold tightly,
keeping me safe from harm.

Take these eyes,
let them see the world
in which we live
as if they were your eyes.

Take these ears,
let them hear the world
and all its fears
as if they were your ears.

May our lives
reflect our faith,
being generous
in giving,
and grateful
in receiving,
being a blessing
as we are blessed.

Open our ears to hear
your gentle voice
call out to us.
Open our eyes to see
your guiding hand
held out for us.

Forgive our lack of attention
as the world we live upon
so openly sings your praise,
in the joyful choral offering
that greets us every day.

Teach us compassion, Lord.
Help us to see this world
through your eyes of love
and the people within
as brothers and sisters
rather than refugees
and economic migrants
looking for a better life
who have no rightful place
in the country where we live.
It will not be easy, Lord
but these are your children
and we should love them too.

Whenever love
holds out its hand
or speaks its name,
may seeds be sown
that, in your time,
will germinate.

You gave to us a garden
that would provide
water for us to drink,
food that we might eat,
sun to bring us warmth,
clouds to give us shade,
rain that seed might grow,
mountains for us to climb,
oceans we can explore.
You gave to us each other,
that we might know
companionship, and
in caring for your garden
walk within it hand in hand,
in fellowship with you.
Gracious God, forgive us
for the damage that we cause
to this world and to each other,
when we forget both gift and giver
and claim ownership for self.


Awaken our senses, Lord,
to the beauty in this world;
how many shades of green
exist within a country scene,
the cheerful song of nightingale,
a brightly painted butterfly,
gentle breeze, trickling stream,
lapping waves, sun going down,
the joy of music, children's play,
lovers embracing, baby's cry.
Awaken our senses, Lord,
to the beauty in this world.

Protect us, Lord,
in a world that would absorb us.
Empower us, Lord,
in a world that would ignore us.

Spirit of peace
blow through this world.
Spirit of light
your brightness shown.
Spirit of love
warm hearts grown cold.
Spirit of truth
your word made known.

## 2 : JOURNEYING TOGETHER

God of the journey,
may you be both
traveling companion
and mountain guide
on this, our daily walk;
lest unprepared
or ill-equipped
our feet should stumble
on uneven ground,
or clouds obscure
the destination
that we so long to see.

God's word be the fuel
God's Spirit the spark,
God's love the oxygen
within which a flame
might be ignited
deep in your heart,
and daily kept alight.

May the default setting
of our hearts be always
switched to generosity.

Forgive us when we forget
how much you desire
our involvement
in the unfolding of your plans,
when rather than be an
active participant
we are content to be the
passive bystander
often heard to grumble
that nothing seems to get done.
Forgive us, and involve us,
Loving God, we pray!

Awesome God,
to you belongs our worship,
the sweet melody in our hearts
that infuses all we are
and everything we do.
May it resound in this place
and wherever we go,
that the melody we share
through our words and lives
might become the song
that this world sings.
To your praise and glory.

Bless us with love
in sensing your arms
reaching to embrace us.
What is it, Loving God
that defines us as human,
if not that inbuilt desire
to reach out and touch
the hand of our Creator?
Not gaining knowledge,
intellectual argument,
or scientific progress,
but allowing ourselves
to be as you created us,
hearts open to worship.

Bless us with strength
when faith is wounded
by the world around us.

Bless us with patience
when our prayers are
seemingly unanswered.

Bless us with peace
when daily schedules
start to overwhelm us.

Bless us with joy
in quiet moments
and simple pleasures.

Give wisdom to all those
leading school assemblies;
inspire their teaching,
enliven their presentation,
and in those precious moments
open the eyes of children
to the possibility of a God
who loves them as they are
yet desires for them much more.
Lord, may seeds of faith be sown
that in days to come might grow
and, when the season's right,
blossom and yield such precious fruit.

Be in my hands today Lord,
in my greeting of a stranger,
the embracing of a friend,
supporting those who stumble,
my generosity.

Be in my hands today Lord,
as I potter in the garden,
write a poem or dream a book,
demonstrate the gifts I'm given,
my creativity.

Be in my hands today Lord.

Father in heaven,
your will be done
in my life today,
words I say,
places I go,
people I meet,
decisions I make,
grace that I bring,
my offering.
Father in heaven,
your will be done
in my life today.

We thank you, Gracious God
for Hallelujah moments.

Those turning a corner
and meeting a long-lost friend
moments.
Those climbing a mountain
and standing in awe of the view
moments.
Those wiping of tears
from our eyes as a baby is born
moments.
Those welcoming back
a prodigal child into our arms
moments.
Those answers to prayer
at times when we feel totally helpless
moments.
Those sighs of relief
at the end of a dear friend's suffering
moments.

For these and all
Hallelujah moments,
we thank you, Gracious God.

Grant us, Lord, a spirit of generosity
that goes beyond both rich and poor
and the giving of our hard-earned cash,
to the investment of our hearts and lives
into your more profitable plan,
demonstrated by your own Son,
developed for the good of everyone.

May we, in faith,
see this world
through your eyes,
hear this world
through your ears,
touch this world
through your hands
and bless this world
through your grace.


May we hear your glorious whisper
breaking through into this day -
in our loneliness and fellowship,
on mountaintop or factory floor,
through noisy streets or countryside,
wherever we might be with you.
May we hear your glorious whisper
breaking through into this day.
Gracious God, in so many ways
this day is a mystery unfolding
for we do not know what it will bring
or what might be expected from us,
and so we offer both to you -
the day that we walk into
and the tasks that we shall face,
that both might be blessed
by your presence and grace.

For all whose journey
has only just begun,
who tread carefully
and heavy laden
along unfamiliar paths,
seeking guidance
from fellow travellers,
fearful of losing their way,
speed their journey, Lord,
keep them from harm,
and bring them safely
into their promised land,
your Kingdom where,
at last unburdened,
they might find their rest in you.


Another week unfolds, Lord,
and we make our choice
to embrace
or walk past
the challenges it brings.
So as we close the door
and begin our daily
journeying with you,
be with us, Lord,
use us as only you
can use us,
that through your grace
we might bring
your blessing
into someone's life
today.

When travelling is hard;
mountains to climb,
rivers to cross,
storms that assail,
and in our own strength
we know that we shall fail,
Lord, reach out your hand
to guide us safely,
and without stumbling,
toward our journey's end.


For all who will make
difficult decisions today,
affecting themselves,
their family and friends,
grant wisdom, courage,
and the faith to know
that whatever may change,
your love for us will not -
on that rock we can depend.


Grant us, Lord, a spirit of generosity
that goes beyond both rich and poor
and the giving of our hard-earned cash,
to the investment of our hearts and lives
into your more profitable plan,
demonstrated by your own Son,
developed for the good of everyone.

In this your beautiful
but fragile world,
bless those
who dedicate their lives
to its care,
who within their hearts
have a passion
to protect its oceans,
forests, plants
and creatures,
who are stewards
of this world
that is our home;
this world,
created by your hand,
given life by your breath,
- a precious place.
This, your gift to us;
its waters refreshing,
its soil providing,
its air sustaining.
In this your beautiful
but fragile world,
bless those
who dedicate their lives
to its care.

Release the gifts within us, Lord
that through fear or hesitation
we have yet to acknowledge or use,
that we might become the Church
you always wanted us to be,
a listening, caring, creative people,
a healing, giving and praying people
filled with the Spirit of love and grace,
your living body here in this place.

Be the wisdom that I hear,
the words that I shall speak,
the love my life reveals
and the song that my heart sings.

For the miracle of life
waiting patiently
within the seed
I sow today -
promising flower,
vegetable, fruit or tree,
Creator God, I thank you!

For creativity expressed
in so many forms
we give you thanks.
For artists who
with simple brushstrokes
capture the essence
of a beautiful scene;
composers who
interpret the music
playing in their souls
into notes on a page;
writers who
with skilful use of words
transport our minds
into another place,
and, like Michelangelo,
those who can
release the angel
inside a block of stone.
For creativity expressed
in so many forms
we give you thanks.

Lord,  should this life fall apart,
remind me that you are an expert
in the art of restoration.

God around us,
God within us,
in our waking,
in our rising,
in our walking,
in our working,
in our thinking,
in our talking,
in our giving,
in our buying,
in our eating,
in our drinking,
in our reading,
in our praying,
in our resting,
in our sleeping.
God around us,
God within us,
this, and every day.


As we journey together
in the footsteps of faith
may we never lose
our sense of direction,
keep eyes focussed
upon our destination,
drink from the well
and eat of the bread
that will bring us life,
and hold out our hand
to any who may falter
or stumble along the way.

In a world full of complexity,
technology and distraction,
speak to us, Creator God
through the beauty of simplicity;
in rising sun and starlit skies,
gentle breeze, flowers, trees,
mountain tops and sacred places,
birds singing, children's laughter,
street musicians, smiling faces,
watching as the world goes by.
Speak to us, Creator God
through the beauty of simplicity
and fill our hearts with joy.

For all who face
this working day
with trepidation,
fearful of decisions
that must be taken,
anxious of outcomes
affecting others;
grant peace of mind,
clarity of thought
and in equal measure
strength and compassion.

Reveal yourself
dear Lord, this day
in the special places
where we can be alone.
Reveal yourself
in the busy places
where noise is all around.
Reveal yourself
in the smiling faces
of friends and family.
Reveal yourself
in the sullen faces
of people passing by.
Reveal yourself
dear Lord, this day
and by your grace
bless this beautiful
but fragile world with joy.

For those struggling
on their journey, Lord,
offer your steady hand
over the rough terrain
they are facing today,
and let them drink
of your living water,
pure and refreshing,
soothing, restoring
the weariest of souls.

Bless our children
as they set out
along the journey
of life and faith;
and parents also,
as they equip
these explorers
and offer guidance,
survival training
for travellers
who, distracted,
might lose their way
and need to know
that your hand,
as well as theirs,
is never far away.


When the journey
through each day
becomes a struggle,
and we wonder
how much further
there is to go,
your gentle voice
can still be heard:
'Sit where you are,
for I am there,
rest once more
in my embrace.'
For your presence
along life's road,
wherever we might be,
we thank you, Lord.

May we find,
within this day
and all it brings,
the noises
and the things
that distract us,
a space,
a pause,
a silence
to be embraced,
an alone-ness
to be sought,
where we can,
if for a moment,
be at peace,
with ourselves,
and with you.

May I never consider
my voice too quiet
to be heard,
my eyes too weak
to discern,
my hands too frail
to be used
my feet too slow
to follow.
For the very least
in your kingdom
are precious indeed!
Amen

(Matthew 11:11)

Grant us space, Lord
within this busy day
to simply rest awhile
in your presence,
whether in the heart
of the countryside,
the comfort
of café chair,
the bustle
of a busy street,
or wherever we might be -
that we might practice
the gentle art of listening.


Declutter our hearts
of all that speaks
of self, and in the space
that this creates
may your love reside,
and others know
they too are welcome.

Trust is not easy, Lord,
for in trusting someone
we ourselves become
vulnerable.
That which we share,
be it joy or sorrow,
past or present,
responsibilities,
emotion, passion -
in the handing over,
that which is dear to us
might become
damaged or abused.
To some this is a real fear.
To some this is a line
which is difficult to cross.
We can trust you, who
in vulnerability
opened your heart
and bled for us
pure love;
but in trusting others
we might need your help.
For all who struggle, Lord,
grant freedom from fear
and a willingness
to accept the risk
of opening life's door
that other might come in.

We pray for those in government,
at local and national level,
that they might use the power
granted to them wisely
and for the common good;
building a society that is both
compassionate and inclusive,
where people are no longer faces
but start to become neighbours,
and towns become communities
caring and supporting one another.


May we know you well enough
to be able to express
within our prayers
the doubts and uncertainties
that often trouble us,
and those distractions
that get between us,
and be confident
in the knowledge
that you understand,
having walked this path before,
and so walk alongside us,
never more than a heartbeat away,
eternally available
to draw us closer, once more, to you.

God of harvest,
gardener supreme,
you place us at the centre ,
feed us, equip us and
having provided for us
look to a different harvest,
a fruitfulness of lives
in service to you
and others.
God of harvest,
feed us,
prune us,
harvest us,
that our lives
might bring glory to you.

God of light and God of night,
Creator of seed and mountain,
raindrop and fountain,
We bring our offering of praise.

God of right and God of might,
Lover of child and childless,
rich and homeless,
We bring our offering of praise.

We bless you,
God of Seed and Harvest
Provider of our daily bread
And we bless each other
That the beauty of this world
And the love that created it
Might be expressed though our lives
And be a blessing to others
Now and always



Bread of Life, you feed us
through word and sacrament.
The bread we share
a remembrance
of your presence with us.
Strengthen us for service,
that seeds we sow
in fertile places
might grow and flourish,
that food we share
in fellowship
might nourish and revive,
that words we share
in our daily walk
might glorify your name.
Bread of Life, you feed us
through word and sacrament
that we might feed others.
Blessed be your name!

Help us spring clean, Lord,
as we sort through so much clutter,
discarding the unwanted,
clearing long-abandoned cobwebs,
dusting in every corner,
cleaning where it shows and maybe
even where it doesn't,
finding hidden treasures
that we thought were lost forever
in our spiritual as well as daily lives.
Help us spring clean, Lord,
before continuing this year, refreshed.

The going can seem tough
as we leave the valley floor
to take the way-marked track
winding up this mountainside;
and when stones beneath our feet
cause us to stumble
and storm clouds gather,
we feel, suddenly, unprepared.
Then we are thankful, Lord
for travelling companions
who encourage us
to see the journey through,
and discover we can lend a hand
to those who struggle as we do.
For this pilgrimage called Life,
and the joy that all will find
as we reach our destination,
Lord of the journey, we give you thanks.

By your Spirit enable us
to take up our cross and follow.
By your Spirit enable us
to speak your word freely.
By your Spirit enable us
to stand up against injustice.
By your Spirit enable us
to bring hope to the downhearted.
By your Spirit enable us
to bring peace from conflict.
By your Spirit enable us
to bring joy into this world.
By your Spirit enable us
to be your hands, your voice,
your willing servants,
wherever you might take us.

Lord, take the raw materials -
often rusty, sometimes damaged -
of which we are composed,
and with your hands
and by your Spirit
create from them
something beautiful to see.

Spirit of mercy
raise us up when faith is weak.
Spirit of freedom
loose the chains that hold us back.
Spirit of power
be the strength we need each day.
Spirit of grace
bless the hands that do your work.
Spirit of wisdom
give us words to change this world.

In the sometimes bleak and windswept
places that our journeying might take us
yours are the sure and steadfast feet
that have walked this way before;
yours the hands that support the weak
and carry them across rough terrain,
yours the calm and encouraging words
enabling us with renewed confidence
to increase our stride and reach the peak.
God of the journey, be our guide
along this pilgrimage that we call life.

Breath of God
blow through this life,
dispelling the clutter
of debris and dust
that has gathered over time,
and creating within
something new,
a sacred place,
a temple fit for you.


For those who have yet to know
deep in their hearts the Father's love,
fall and be raised to their feet
by the touch of a Saviour's hand,
or feel the Spirit bringing peace
to a restlessness in their soul;
reveal yourself, O Lord, we pray,
to young and old, to rich and poor,
open your arms, welcome them home.


Loving God, protect all those
whose declaration of faith
also puts their lives in danger;
and who, like your disciples,
refuse to take the easy path
of unbelief because they know
deep in their hearts the truth
that the cross we bear today
becomes, through Jesus Christ,
a crown we share tomorrow.

We thank you for all that has been,
the experiences that have shaped us
and made us the people who we are,
vulnerable, but valuable in your service.
We trust you for all that is to come,
the opportunities that await us
as every day we step out in faith,
willingly, for your Spirit is also with us.

Your footsteps are not easy to follow,
for they lead not only to green pastures
where we find nourishment and rest,
but also desert and wilderness places
where we are vulnerable and alone,
and crowded and uncomfortable spaces
where we feel threatened and distressed.
Your footsteps are not easy to follow,
but you have walked this way before
and are never far from any one of us,
your Spirit guiding and instructing,
your arm supporting, your love supplying,
on this necessary path we tread.

Forgive us when we fail
to live the faith we speak;
when we talk of sharing
yet hold on tight to what is ours;
when we talk of freedom
while so many are still in chains;
when we talk of equality
and continue to discriminate;
when we talk of forgiveness
yet in our hearts cannot forgive.
Open our eyes, open our hearts,
that others, through our lives,
might see the reality of your love.

God of the moment
be in our busyness,
the don't have time
for anyone moments,
the running around
chasing our tail moments.

God of the moment
be in our solitude,
the time to take stock
and quiet moments,
the stilling our minds
and prayerful moments.

God of the moment
be with us, always.

Lord God, Master Craftsman;
from the uneven stone
and raw material
that our lives provide,
create something useful,
a functional building,
a beautiful building,
one that can stand up
against the fiercest storm,
and within which can be seen
something of the character
of its builder and creator.


Lord bless our relaxation;
grant peace in our lives
for both body and mind,
relief from distraction,
quality time, set aside
for family and friends,
but also for ourselves.


Christ, be the light
shining brightly before us.
Christ, be the song
in our hearts every day.
Christ, be the love
flowing into and from us.
Christ, be the shield
that protect us from harm.

Be the rock
that we stand firm upon.
Be the light
we can depend upon.
Be the bread
that we can feed upon.
Be the path
we choose to walk upon.
Be the truth
we base our lives upon.


May we tread lightly
through this world today,
listening to its many voices,
observing its many faces,
sensing its many problems
and praying, Lord, for answers.


Be with us when faith is weak,
the road is hard to see,
tiredness overwhelms us
and it's hard to carry on.
Be with us when faith is strong,
the road is effortless,
beauty surrounds us
and hearts overflow with song.
In our weakness and our strength
be with us, Lord. Be with us.

Circle us with your love,
enfold us in its warm embrace.
Circle us with your peace,
enfold us in its warm embrace.
Circle us with your joy,
enfold us in its warm embrace.
Circle us, and in this enfolding
we shall be one, in fellowship with you.

Bless the hands that share your work
Bless the minds that know your ways
Bless the lips that speak your word
Bless the hearts that sing your praise

Encourage, Lord,
those whose hearts
are fixed on you,
and whose lives
are lived for others,
for with such stones
your kingdom's walls
will be made strong.

Give us courage, Lord,
not just to walk away
from difficult issues
and those hard to answer
questions we are asked,
for in doing so our faith
is always weakened
and opportunity is lost.
Grant us the humility
to say, 'I don't know',
and discover together
within your Word,
and by your Holy Spirit,
the answers that we seek.

We seek forgiveness,
having forgotten
how to be thankful
for having enough
to satisfy our needs,
tempted by a world
that tries so hard
to satisfy our wants.
Forgive our greed,
give us thankful hearts,
and a generous spirit.

# 3 : THE WIDER WORLD

We pray for all those for whom
each day is a continuing struggle
to find suitable employment -
searching for vacancies,
filling endless forms,
attending interviews,
rejection letters
or no responses at all.
Back to square one,
making ends meet
on limited means,
trips to the food bank,
second hand clothes.
Lord of compassion
bring hope where there is none,
and opportunity to those
who long to be productive
and contributing members
of their families and neighbourhood.

Under the warmth
of the summer sun
the world awakes and blossoms
into unimaginable colour.
A garden created for us to enjoy,
and within it planted
such variety of flowers, grass and trees.
You needed no horticultural training
to plan your colour scheme,
to recommend variety or design.
Your garden is perfect,
its colours harmonious,
its scale immense,
spoilt only by the clumsiness
of those who tend it.

Grant me opportunity, Lord
within this busy day
to find time for someone
who needs a sympathetic ear,
bring a word of peace
to a life that is full of stress,
ease somebody's load
and let them know I'm there.
Grant me opportunity, Lord
to be of service
both to others, and to you.

Help us to see others
through the lens of your eyes,
that we might see beyond
the outward appearance,
and our own prejudice,
to the person who lies within -
and beyond the bluster,
bitterness, aggression,
reticence, joy or sadness,
all those attributes that seem
somehow to define them,
to the image of the divine
that was crafted deep within them
at the moment of their creation.
Help us to see others
through the lens of your eyes,
it will make such a difference.

Make us a blessing today,
that through our words
and in our actions
something of your love
might be discerned
in a receptive heart,
and a seed sown
that in your good time
will be encouraged to grow.

Make us a people
worthy of your kingdom, Lord
who are extravagant in praise,
diligent in prayer,
generous in service,
slow to anger, swift to love,
a blessing and a burning light
within this dark and fragile world
Make us a people
worthy of your kingdom, Lord.

Thank you, Lord
for showing us that love
has no boundaries or end
but listens, has patience,
compassion, grace
and gives without counting cost.
Thank you for granting us
a heart for those you love
and a willingness
to step out in faith
and service.
Thank you, Lord
for showing us true love
can be ours to know and give.

Help me Lord, to accept
those whose theology
is different from mine,
embrace them in love
as fellow travellers
on this journey of faith,
and have the humility
to admit that even I
may not always be right!

Open our eyes
to the beauty within
an artist's brush,
a writer's pen.
Open our ears
to the glory within
a major chord
and symphony.
Open our minds
to the truth within
a seed that's sown
and thoughts set free.
Open our hearts
Creative God
to creativity!

I pray for the people
behind the faces
I shall pass today.
The cheerful faces,
peaceful faces,
carefree faces,
bewildered faces,
wounded faces,
anxious faces,
resentful faces,
angry faces,
deep in thought faces,
difficult to read faces.
Bless these people, Lord,
your precious people.
May they feel your presence
and hear your whisper
within their busyness
and loneliness today.

Use these hands
to carry the burden.
Use this voice
to carry your word.

For difficult decisions
that must be made today
affecting the lives of others
in hospitals, homes and workplaces,
grant courage and compassion
in equal measure,
and for those who are affected
bring an unexpected peace,
and understanding
of the road that they must follow.

As this day unfolds may we know
God's presence as we wake,
God's guidance as we walk,
God's wisdom as we speak,
God's patience as we listen,
God's strength as we endure,
God's joy as we reach out,
God's love as we forgive,
God's provision as we eat,
God's stillness as we pray,
God's peace within our sleep.

Gracious God, may we know
the gift of generosity
and the joy that it can bring.
Generous with time
helping those who need a hand.
Generous with care
being there when times are bad.
Generous with wealth
thankful that we have so much.
Generous with hope
reassuring those who fear.
Generous with prayer
when there's illness or distress.
Generous with love
giving without counting cost.
Gracious God, may we know
the gift of generosity
and the joy that it can bring
both to those who receive
and to the one who gives.

Bless those loved ones of yours
who I will pass on my journey today;
buskers strumming half-remembered tunes,
the beggar sitting quietly with upturned hat,
teenagers hanging round street corners,
coffee drinkers getting their first fix,
shoppers looking for early bargains,
market traders setting up their goods.
Strangers to me, but loved by you,
be known to them, Gracious Lord, today.

Help us in our fellowship
to pray before we meet
think before we speak
consider before we act
and embrace before we part.

For all who are called
to be your image-bearers,
your saints in cities,
towns and villages,
carrying the divine torch
within hearts and lives
so others might be warmed
and glimpse the light within.
For all who are called
not just to be followers
but doers of your word.
For us, the church,
your body here on earth,
called to be saints
and image-bearers
wherever we might be,
commissioned into service,
sanctified by you.
Bless us, and any
whose lives we touch
as we carry your precious love
into a fragile world today.

We pray for families
who, for various reasons
find themselves
living beyond their means,
unable to provide
even life's essentials
without borrowing more,
despairing more,
sinking deeper into debt.
Oh Father, that we might be
a compassionate nation,
more ready to give
than take away,
more ready to love
than to condemn,
more ready to lend
a helping hand,
working together
for the common good
of all your children
within this land.
Through Jesus Christ,
who took the little
that was available
and shared it such
that all were fed,
this we pray. Amen

Bless us with strength
when faith is wounded
by the world around us.

Bless us with patience
when our prayers are
seemingly unanswered.

Bless us with peace
when daily schedules
start to overwhelm us.

Bless us with joy
in quiet moments
and simple pleasures.

Bless us with love
in sensing your arms
reaching to embrace us.

Gracious God, may we know
the gift of generosity
and the joy that it can bring.

For all who we love,
both family and friends,
be that constant presence
in their daily lives
with whom they can share
both joys and sorrows,
and know they can turn to
in times of trouble.
Be the rock they choose
to build their lives upon,
that sure foundation
on which they can depend.

When I ask someone,
"How are you?"
may it cease to be
a throwaway greeting
and swiftly move on,
but be spoken with love
and compassion,
showing genuine interest,
and leaving space
in my life for theirs
should the answer be
"Do you really want to know?"

Please Lord,
may the seed
we sow this day
find good soil
within hearts
already warmed
by your love,
and in your time
become fruitful,
for your glory.


Help us see your image
in the faces of those
we pass today;
politician,
financier,
neighbour,
policeman,
factory worker,
security guard,
refuse collector,
single mother,
homeless,
beggar,
prostitute,
thief.
Help us see
as you do
not just a person
but the potential within.

Let my eyes
be your eyes
sharing compassion
warmth and love.
Let my hands
be your hands
bringing healing
with their touch.
Let my ears
be your ears
listening where
there is need.
Let my words
be your words
bringing comfort
joy and peace.


Encircle us with love
as we journey into this day
Fill us to overflowing
that wherever we might walk
your love might radiate from us
and warm the hearts of those
whose lives we touch
Blessing them and blessing us.

Lord, bless the many
who, over the years
have been a blessing to us;
who introduced us to you
and nurtured a new-found faith;
who were encouragers
to persevere when times were tough;
who were available,
a hand to hold, a listening ear,
and who continue
to remember us in prayer.
May we, so richly blessed
be imitators of these saints,
drawing others into your presence,
kneeling with them at your feet,
being with them on the journey,
encouraging new life.

What a privilege to serve,
to share your love
through word and action.
What a joy to know
that what we say
can bring change in others.
What a blessing to see,
hearts touched
by the riches of your Grace.
What a harvest to be,
when seeds we sow
produce fruitfulness.

It is a wonderful truth
that you have already walked
the path that we now follow
known hardship, temptation and suffering
And with that knowledge deep in our hearts
we can follow you in confidence
and when difficulties arise
listen for your footfall.



May we become
change-makers
in our neighbourhood,
hands of love
reaching out
where there is need,
sowing seeds
where one day
flowers begin to bloom.
May we become
change-makers
in our daily lives,
standing up,
speaking out
for what is right,
confronting
all that's not
in this our fragile world.
May our voice
become the wind
that those in power
cannot ignore.

As we close the door behind us
and venture out into this day,
reveal to us the neighbours
who live just along our street,
who smile each time we pass
but remain strangers in our midst.
May we never be so busy
that we ignore an opportunity
to share even a moment
of our all too precious time,
to exchange a friendly word
or even introduce ourselves,
for through such encounters
and a sharing of our lives,
Your love might be revealed,
and a seed of faith be scattered
into new and fertile ground.

We bring to you those
for whom every day
has become a struggle,
another mountain to climb,
and often a little steeper
than one climbed yesterday.
Gracious God, bring relief,
a gentler path to follow,
time for healing, time for rest.
Strengthen body and soul, we ask.

God of all I am,
God of all I will become,
be in the words I speak
in every conversation,
the hands I offer
in service and dedication,
the footsteps I follow
from beginning to destination.
God of all I am,
God of all I will become,
be with me always.
Bless our families;
mothers, fathers,
daughters, sons.
Protect them
from all that might harm.
Prosper them
in times of hardship.
Instruct them
in the ways of goodness.
Prepare them
for both joy and sorrow.
Unite them
within your arms of love.
Daughters, sons,
mothers, fathers,
bless our families
Lord, we pray.

Heal the hurts
deep inside,
that no salve
or medication
can alleviate.
Open hearts,
reach inside
and take away
all that harms -
anguish, fears,
doubts, despairs
lying deep within -
and in their place
leave hope and love.

## 4 : WHEN LIFE IS HARD

For those who walk
more slowly
through this world
than in the days
when they were young,
may each step
be made lighter
and their joy be greater
for seeing beauty
in little things
that the hurrying pass by.

(A prayer for those with dementia)

Memory fades,
and recollections
become hazy clouds,
fading outlines
of strangers' faces
and forgotten places.
Even the familiar,
loved ones and names
that once tripped lightly
off the tongue
cause confusion,
in what seems
a cruel dismantling
of a life once lived.
Compassionate God,
for all who live in fear
of what they might become,
and those already walking
down this lonely road
we call dementia
grant them peace.
May each moment,
however brief,
be filled with joy
not sorrow,
and your love be seen
through those
who care for these,
your loved and fragile people.

We pray for those who find
difficulty in remembering;
for whom once-familiar faces
are becoming strangers,
and treasured memories
disappear from memory's store.
Lord, grant understanding
to those who care for these
your vulnerable children,
and dignity to those
who suffer in this way.
May they know and feel
your love surround them
and every moment,
though soon forgotten
be a moment filled with joy.

Lord, help us accept with grace
that this journey of life
is limited both by time
and the process of growing old.
May we leave the path
a little easier to follow,
less overgrown with weeds
or thorns likely to cause pain,
an encouragement for others
to step out in faith with you.

Thank you, Lord
for the wisdom of age,
such a valuable guide
for those walking
unfamiliar
or hazardous routes.

God of compassion and grace,
we pray for all those who,
through age and infirmity
find themselves imprisoned
within the loneliness of home,
watching a world outside
that once had their
full involvement
increasingly pass them by.
Be with and bless them, Lord,
along with family and carers
calling through the week to help.
May they know that they are loved,
still precious in your sight,
and feel your arms support them
in the day and through the night.

Thank you, Lord, for those
who have served you faithfully
throughout their lives
and now, with advancing years
and confined within their homes,
are content to spend time
in prayerful intercession
for the town in which  they live,
and for those of us more able
than they now find themselves
to continue with the task
of building your kingdom
in these hearts and in this place.
Bless their faithfulness
and the offering of their prayers,
Gracious Lord, we pray.

For all with low self-esteem,
who lack confidence
and undervalue their worth
within your kingdom,
draw close to them, Lord,
open their hearts and minds
to the real valuation
you place upon their lives,
and by your Holy Spirit
fill their emptiness within
with the fullness of your love.

Gracious God, bring healing,
peace and calm to those
troubled with depression
and such health issues
that make it impossible
to open the front door
and welcome each new day,
summon up the energy
to make their way to work
or school, meet up with friends,
communicate with family
or address the things that make
each morning so difficult to face.
Wrap them in your embrace,
circle them with love
and bring restoration
and completeness
to lives that are broken,
that these, your children,
might become the people
you long for them to be.


Raise us up, Lord
when we are weary,
encourage us
when we are low;
speak to our hearts
by your sweet Spirit,
and lead us, Lord
where we should go.

For all who woke this morning
to the familiar embrace of pain
in muscles, joints and nerves,
that make each day a mountain
they must try once more to climb.
We pray of course for healing,
but also strength to persevere,
and faith that makes a mountain
so much lower than it seems.

May the lonely
know your love
embracing them.
May the anxious
know your peace
surrounding them.
May the weary
know your strength
refreshing them.
May the tearful
know your hand
supporting them.
May the suffering
know your touch
restoring them.
On this and all days.
So be it, Lord.

Healing God,
we bring to you
the aches and pain
endured each day
within our bodies,
that slow us down,
restrict movement
and cause distress.
Pour your Spirit,
that healing oil,
into these muscles,
bones and joints.
Bring freedom
and relief, we ask,
in Jesus' name.


Wherever your children
have woken
to the company
of a familiar
loneliness,
and this day,
like any other,
seem devoid
of meaning or life,
may they know
the continual warmth
of your companionship,
the comfort of your words,
and their daily solitude
be filled with song

Heal the hurts within our lives,
both visible and invisible,
that these broken vessels
might once more be made whole.


God of compassion,
draw near to those who,
even in the midst
of a crowded place,
know only loneliness
and the chill of isolation.
Stand beside them,
friend of the friendless,
lover of the lost,
and in your warm embrace
may they understand
how much they are loved,
and understanding, have peace.


Bring peace, Lord
to the worried.
Bring calm, Lord
to the stressed.
Bring hope, Lord
to the downcast,
and to the tired,
Lord, grant them rest.

For all who woke this morning
to the familiar embrace of pain
in muscles, joints and nerves,
that make each day a mountain
they must try once more to climb.
We pray of course for healing,
but also strength to persevere,
and faith that makes a mountain
so much lower than it seems.

For those who walk
through an enveloping darkness,
obscuring their vision
of a world that would accept
and love them
just as they are;
a darkness
that cannot simply be relieved
by exposure to light
or medication
several times a day;
a darkness
striving for a level of success
that will bring a cure,
where sadness
will be no more.
For those who walk
through the darkness
of depression, dear Lord,
we pray for healing,
wholeness, light,
and the warmth of your embrace.

We bring to you, Lord,
all those for whom home
has gradually become a prison,
whether through infirmity,
isolation or irrational fear;
whose window into the world
is confined to a single street
and the strangers passing by.
Bless carers, neighbours,
and all who keep an eye
on these, your vulnerable people,
and in their solitude
be an ever-present source of comfort,
the one to whom they can turn
without fear of ridicule,
who will love and accept them
just as they are,
and in your time, and theirs
bring healing.

When our faith is weak
grant us wisdom
When our body is weak
grant us strength
When our journey is long
grant us perseverance.

Be a constant presence
in the lives of those
who are lonely,
that certain voice
reminding them
that within solitude
contentment can be found,
and mountaintops revealed
in the most unlikely of places.
Bring comfort, merciful Lord
to all who are fearful of outcomes
for those whom they love,
who wait anxiously for news
that will ease their distress;
parents, children, siblings, friends
feeling helpless, anticipating loss.
Bring comfort, through the love
of those who surround them.
Bring comfort, as your arms
reach out to enfold them.
Bring comfort, dear Lord we pray.

God of peace, be with those
who are anxious today.
Still the water, calm the storm,
reach out your hand
for them to hold, we pray.

We pray for healing and peace
for the stresses and strains
within family relationships.
For couples who have lost
the love that they once had,
and their lives are drifting apart.
For parents who no longer
can control their children,
and are beginning to despair.
For families who struggle
to live within their means
and not slip deeper into debt.
For children who walk into
a more uncertain future
with difficult choices to make.
For the stresses and strains
within family relationships
we pray for healing and peace.




I bring to you my body,
muscle and sinew,
artery and vein.
bone and joint,
the miracle that is me.
I bring to you my brokenness,
and ask for healing
restoration
freedom to be
the person I could be.

May God who shapes us
and breathes life into us
bring restoration where,
through no fault but time,
those joints and muscles
that have worked so well
now seem to cause us pain.
For wholeness, freedom
of movement, and strength
enough for each new day.
Gracious God, we pray.

In the loneliness
of a sitting room,
crowded train,
country lane,
apartment block,
hospital ward,
shopping mall,
production line,
prison cell,
nursing home,
be there, Lord,
in fellowship,
a friend indeed
to those in need.

For all your children
who begin this day
with a heavy heart,
self-doubt, anxiety,
tormented by fear,
living with stress,
may your presence
within their darkness
bring not only light
but understanding
of a love so strong
that can protect us
against the worst
that life can throw,
and in the calm
when storm subsides
still will not let us go.

God of peace, who calmed
the pounding of the waves,
bring stillness to this heart
amidst the storms of life
which threaten all around.
And in the peace, hold out
your hand, that I may safely
find my way from sea to shore.

Be my strength
when I am weary,
be the healing
within my pain,
be my comfort
when I am lonely,
be the delight
that fills my day.

Bless those known to us
who today are suffering
from sickness or infirmity.
Draw close to them, we pray,
heal both mind and body
with your gentle touch,
and pour your Spirit
like a refreshing stream
into every corner of their lives,
restoring them to wholeness

Be our strength when trouble comes
Be our peace when fear assails
Be our light when darkness looms
Be our healing when body fails.

Loving God, be with the lonely,
wherever they happen to be;
sitting quietly within their home,
driving to work, going to school,
walking the dog, catching a train,
in prison, hospital, care home,
office, factory, construction site,
behind the till in a sandwich shop.
Loving God, be with the lonely,
for the lonely are all around us.


God of compassion,
grant peace, we pray
for all those who,
awaiting the results
of diagnostic tests
are fearful
of the consequences
for themselves,
their family and friends.
May they know
deep in their hearts
that certain knowledge
that you are never closer
than in our darkest day,
your light enough
for us to see ahead,
your strength enough
to carry us through.
God of compassion,
grant peace, we pray.

For all who are imprisoned
through sickness or fear,
unable or unwilling
to set foot
beyond the door
of that called home,
where the world beyond
can only be glimpsed
through window pane,
newspaper print
or TV screen -
Bring wholeness
into these fragile lives,
bring release
even for a little while,
bring healing
of body, mind and soul.
May the door
which confines them
be opened wide,
and the beauty
within their lives
become a blessing for us all.

For all who struggle
through storms of life,
physical or spiritual,
we pray for peace,
calmer days,
respite
from gales
that threaten
to overwhelm them.
And when clouds pass
and storm subsides,
may they be given
a firm foundation
for any necessary
restoration,
upon a cornerstone
that can withstand
the fiercest blow.


For carers in this world,
young and old,
whose love, time
and freedom,
sometimes even childhood
is given sacrificially
for one who is in need,
may they know your blessing,
through good days and bad,
and receive as they have given
love in good measure,
flowing as a gentle river
into their hearts and lives.

For lives that seem broken,
lying derelict on the ground
upon which they were built
Lord, bring your restoration.
Raise up that which has fallen,
strengthen all that is weak,
repair damage within and without
and rebuild with stone that can
withstand the fiercest of storms,
that these lives, these temples
where together we reside
might once again reflect
within their windows
your beauty and your grace.

We pray for all whose lives
are consumed by caring
for the long-term needs
of children, parents,
the elderly or infirm
and whose patience,
love and commitment
is sometimes tested
beyond the point of breaking.
Grant them strength, Lord.
Bless them as they give
from that deep well
within their hearts,
and in moments of despair
draw near, and hold them
safe within your loving arms.

God of love and mercy,
embrace all those
whose hearts today
overflow with grief,
unanswered questions
and such a sense of loss.
Grant them space
to express their tears.
Hold them close
through the coming days.


Lord, we commend to you
those who minister daily
to the sick and suffering,
and within hospitals,
hospices and homes
bring words of grace,
peace and comfort
to those who are fearful,
facing treatment, surgery,
or the final days of life.
Grant them strength, Lord
in often harrowing situations
and a faith that can transcend
the endless question, "Why?"
Bless them, Lord, we pray
and all whose lives they touch.
We ask this through Christ alone
who died and is risen
that we might know,
in the midst of our distress,
the true meaning of life and love.

We pray for Chaplains, and all
who today will bring your love
and compassionate words
into hospice and hospital wards
and minister to both sick and dying.
It is a precious gift of the Spirit
to bring your love and peace
into such difficult situations.
Bless those who do this work,
and all to whom they minister,
and though we long for healing,
may they recognise your presence
through the words that are spoken,
and that knowledge bring them peace.


Lord, for all whose lives
are imprisoned by pain,
may they know release.
Where pain is physical,
in mind or body,
bring relief through
your healing touch
and the skill of Doctors.
Where pain is emotional,
through hurt or loss,
bring relief through
your comforting touch
and the love of others.
Lord, for all whose lives
are imprisoned by pain,
may they know release.

Loving God, be with the lonely,
wherever they happen to be;
sitting quietly within their home,
driving to work, going to school,
walking the dog, catching a train,
in prison, hospital, care home,
office, factory, construction site,
behind the till in a sandwich shop.
Loving God, be with the lonely,
for the lonely are all around us.

In the loneliness
of a sitting room,
crowded train,
country lane,
apartment block,
hospital ward,
shopping mall,
production line,
prison cell,
nursing home,
be there, Lord,
in fellowship,
a friend indeed
to those in need.

Thank you for the remembrance
of loved ones no longer with us;
for their inspiring words,
encouragement,
love and support,
an example for us to follow.
May their legacy be seen
in the people we have become,
and may we always be thankful.
Bless those who mourn
the death of relative or friend
and feel that with this loss
their lives are incomplete.

Bless those who mourn,
and fill these empty hearts
with pleasant memories,
the sound of laughter,
sunshine and happier days.

Bless those who mourn,
and heal their brokenness
with the soothing balm
of your gentle touch,
that they might know
shalom, wholeness, peace.

We pray for all whose lives
have been touched by tragedy,
whether by accident
or a deliberate act.
For those who mourn,
immerse them in your love
and lead them through this darkness
into your arms, and light.
For those who comfort,
be in both the words they use
and all that's left unspoken;
fill each heart with love.
We ask this through Jesus Christ,
whose own suffering brought us life,
here and for eternity.

For all those who woke this morning
to the loneliness of bereavement -
the empty bed or chair,
an unaccustomed quietness,
a life now incomplete -
may they know your presence
in the stillness of the day,
and through the love of friends
who offer their condolence.
And in the darker moments
may they reach out to hold your hand
and feel the warmth of the One
who has already passed from death to life
to welcome others into God's Kingdom.

Thank you for the lives
of all those loved ones
who, whilst no longer
walking beside us
or holding our hand
along life's journey
as once they did, live on
in the collective memory
of those they have left behind.
Enjoy their company, Loving God
until we shall meet again.


Bless those who visit
the lonely, confined
within their own homes
by old age, infirmity
or fear of venturing out.
The social workers,
pastoral visitors,
health professionals,
concerned neighbours,
those who bring a smile
and a little time to share,
who demonstrate that every life,
however solitary, is precious.
Bless them with your peace and love.

# 5 : THE WIDER WORLD

Oh, that a busy world
might pause to glance
through Scripture's window
and see within its pages
not just history, prophesy,
signs and wonders,
beautiful poetry
or even controversy;
but simply hands
that from the formless
created a universe,
raised a people,
embraced the poor,
lifted the weak
and, even now,
held out for all to touch
still show the scars
of a Saviour's love.

We pray for the Church,
the children of God
clothed in so many colours
throughout this world.
God's rainbow people!
Beyond the divisions
and within our diversity
may there be found
a unity of purpose
and eagerness
to become image-bearers
of the One we serve,
and, empowered
by the Holy Spirit
be change-makers
in this beautiful
but troubled world.

We pray for young Christians
growing up in a secular world,
that they might be courageous
in standing up for what is right,
unafraid to share their faith
and by your Spirit become
beacons of light and grace.
May they be truly blessed
and become a real blessing
to the families and communities
within which they work and live.

Thank you for the extended family
that is your Church worldwide,
our brothers and sisters in Christ
who we shall never know in this life,
but have an eternity in which to enjoy
their fellowship in the life to come.
May the prayer and worship
that we offer here on earth
rise as a fragrant offering,
to enhance the heavenly chorus
already praising your glorious name.

God of all people,
grant understanding
between those
of many faiths and none;
a mutual respect that goes
beyond personal opinion,
engaging in dialogue
rather than using
the language of aggression
or engendering distrust,
a respect that acknowledges
that we are all of us
actively engaged
in a journey of discovery
for that which we called "Truth"

We bring to you, loving God
this world and all your children
at the start of this new day.
For all who sing out
in praise and worship,
may their lives resound with song.
For those who bring fears
to lay at your feet
grant strength to carry on.
For those without words
but tears in their eyes
enfold them in your love.
For all who cry out
in pain and anguish
bring comfort and release.
We bring to you, loving God
this world and all your children
at the start of this new day,
may we be blessed
and become a blessing,
God of love, we pray.

Shine Lord into the shadows of this world
and by the light of your people dispel the darkness
that this world might glimpse your grace
and seeing it might understand the difference.

For your people, Lord
wherever they might be,
brothers and sisters in Christ
who like us begin this day
with mixed emotions;
hopes and fears,
joys and sorrows,
peace and pain,
anticipation,
Lord, by your Spirit
create lives of faith
from such rough
and fragile stones
and transform us
into the people
we were meant to be,
reflections of your love
that this world,
touched by our lives, can see.


Lord, forgive our prejudice,
our judgement of others,
often based on our assessment
of your point of view,
but seen through our eyes.
We fail to understand
that your mercy and grace
are available to all who will,
in humility, kneel down at your feet,
not simply those for whom
we would give our approval.
Lord, forgive our prejudice.

God bless
the persecuted
and oppressed
God bless
the refugee
and dispossessed.

Barriers fall down
in your kingdom, Lord.
Social class, wealth
and upbringing
count as nothing
in your evaluation
of our potential,
and your love for those
you are pleased to call brother,
sister and family -
your extended family
throughout this world,
in all its shades and diversity.
O that we might also see
beyond outward appearance
and the colour of a skin
to the heart that beats inside;
that within your kingdom
here on earth, Lord,
our own personal barriers
might fall down
and your family grow in love.

For all whose home is shop doorway,
railway arch, overnight hostel,
any temporary dwelling place,
for whom winter is a familiar foe
taking its toll on weak and frail,
bring comfort Lord, through cold nights,
somewhere to sleep, help for the sick;
and bless the saints who leave the warmth
of their own homes to do what they can,
support the weak, feed the hungry,
be your arms embracing the lost.

We come to you, Lord,
for the hungry of this world,
that they might find food to eat.
We come to you, Lord,
for the thirsty of this world,
that they might find water to drink.
We come to you, Lord,
for the homeless of the world
that they might find somewhere to live.
We come to you, Living Water,
Bread of Life, for whom this earth
was but a temporary home,
that these, your precious people
might find within your mercy
and gracious provision
an answer to their needs.

God of compassion and grace
we pray for those on the margins,
who have just enough work,
just enough to eat and drink,
just enough to heat the house,
clothe their children, pay the rent;
just enough, but not enough
to make life easy, or reduce
the stress of unplanned costs,
not enough for holidays
or days out with the kids,
just enough, but not enough,
who are just living, but life is tough.
We pray for those on the margins,
God of compassion and grace.

Forgive us, Lord.
Your footsteps
are not always
easy to discern,
but your word
reveals a path
for us to follow,
and your hand
is always there
for us to hold.

One in eight, Lord,
will eat just less than enough
than their body requires
before they sleep tonight,
and every night.
One in eight, Lord,
will eat just less than enough
to feed body and mind,
and succumb to illnesses
they cannot fight.
One in eight, Lord,
will eat just less than enough.
As our plates are cleaned
and needs satisfied,
remind us, Lord.


This is a strange world
when one billion children
are living in poverty
and one billion adults
earn less than $1.25 a day
whilst around us
people complain
of crowded shops,
nowhere to park
and websites down,
whilst spending
all they have and more
on the appropriately named
Black Friday.

As we turn the tap
to fill our glass
help us remember
those who walk miles
this and every day
to find clean water.

Lord of heaven and earth
of all nations and peoples
all faiths and no faith
reveal yourself
to those who are suffering,
reveal yourself
to all who are refugees,
reveal yourself
to those who are powerful,
reveal yourself
to all who are powerless,
reveal yourself
to ordinary people
in their everyday lives,
that this world
might reflect your love
and your glory.

Today Lord, we bring to you
the forgotten people
who were TV headlines
just a month or two ago;
who are still suffering,
still fleeing for their lives,
still dying for lack
of medical provision,
still seeing their world
crumbling into dust
beneath tired feet,
but whose plight
has been downgraded
to make room
for more recent barbarity.
Lord, we bring to you
this fragile world,
its precious people,
its suffering people,
its forgotten people,
made beautifully in your image
and still crying out for help.

You are God
of the refugee,
the oppressed
and dispossessed.
You are God
of the weak,
the starving
and suffering.
You are God
who asks for
justice
like a flowing river,
goodness
as a sparkling stream,
love
that is seen in action.
Forgive us,
challenge us,
change us,
God of love, we pray.

For all whose lives have been cut short
through the violence of others,
and mothers, fathers, brothers and sisters
mourn their loss and count the cost,
enfold them with your gentle Spirit,
walk with them through their grief,
and may violence not beget violence
but give birth to righteousness and peace.

Father God, we bring to you
the children of this world
for whom employment
rather than education
is a daily experience;
where childhood is taken
and young lives endangered
in often hazardous conditions.
Strengthen the voice of those
whose cry is to see justice
for the vulnerable in this world;
and bless those young children,
for to such, you remind us,
belongs the Kingdom of Heaven.

We remember the many
who are imprisoned
simply because they choose
to speak the truth,
stand up against injustice
and expose that which is wrong
within the country they call home -
very much as you once did.
Bless the courage of their actions,
and loose the chains that bind them,
Lord of liberty and life, we pray.

For all young people
whose childhood
has been exchanged
for bonded slavery
sweatshops or mines,
domestic servitude,
sex trade or crime,
we pray for liberty.
Give them a voice
that this world can hear,
a cry for justice
that will not be silenced
until chains are broken
and these, your children
are finally set free.

Hear the voices in this world
who are crying out for war,
showing no regard for life,
or understanding of the love
poured out upon a cross
for the sake of all who live
upon this garden we call earth.
Work within their hearts, Lord,
clear away the weeds of hate
and create instead a fertile soil
within which a seed or two of love
might one day germinate and grow.

We pray, Lord, for all
who suffer persecution
because of their faith,
and find themselves
without employment,
education or worse -
forced to leave the place
where they belong
and with their families
become refugees
within a foreign land.
Lord, you have walked
the path they follow,
to suffering and beyond,
be with them in their sorrow,
strengthen and lead them
to a brighter tomorrow
and a future filled with hope

We do not know why
a suicide bomber
chooses selfishly
to sacrifice their life
and others in the name
of the god they serve,
and can only add
our tears to yours,
whose selfless sacrifice
was made for all,
that powers of darkness
shall eventually be overcome.

Embrace this fragile world
within your loving arms,
as a mother would a child,
protecting it from harm.


God of wholeness,
where bodies are broken
through illness,
injury or chronic pain,
bring comfort,
relief and healing.
If through stress
of conflict and fleeing homes,
bring hope, strength
and restoration.
Where bodies are broken
through torture,
abuse or false imprisonment,
bring freedom
faith and justice.
Whether through doctors,
peacemakers,
politicians, miracles
or the actions
of ordinary people.
Through your great love and mercy
hear our prayer.

We pray for today's victims of conflict;
the mothers, fathers, sons and daughters
who face a daily struggle to survive
the bombs, missiles and sniper's bullet,
lack of food, water or medical help -
these human pawns in a game of chance,
played by politicians with no regard,
it would appear, for the sanctity of life.
God of Justice we pray both for victims
and perpetrators that this might end,
along with the fear, hatred and prejudice
that combine to start so many wars.

Lighten the darkness
that has wrapped itself
around this world,
a shadow of self-interest
that places the value
and needs of others
below those of 'me'.
In its place may love
shine its stronger light,
burning away the shadows,
warming hearts grown cold,
and remaining as a lamp
within those hearts and lives
that cannot be extinguished,
for it has its source in you.

Grant us a willingness
to speak out for the weak
and vulnerable.
Grant us a readiness
to point out the corrupt
and indefensible.

For children of all nations
forced through disease or hardship
to become mature beyond their years
and provide for the needs of family,
bless and empower them
and bring healing and compassion
to those for whom they care.
For those who walk
the path of suffering
for the sake of your name,
who are persecuted
and oppressed
yet will not lay aside
something so precious
for a temporary peace,
choosing instead
to walk with faith
through temporary
darkness
to brighter days,
glorious days ahead.
Lord, bring your blessing
on these your children,
for to such, you have said
belongs the kingdom of God.

We pray for all who
because of their faith
find themselves excluded
from participating within
the society in which they live;
for whom work is hard to find,
family a struggle to feed,
insults follow them around
and normal life is sacrificed
for the One they choose to serve.
Give them a voice, Lord
for within your kingdom
there are no outsiders.
Give them strength, Lord
for those times when faith
is tested to the limit.
Bless them with hope, Lord
for to such you have said
belongs the kingdom of heaven.

(Matthew 5:10,11)

Whenever love
holds out its hand
or speaks its name,
may seeds be sown
that, in your time,
will germinate.

We pray for today's victims of conflict;
the mothers, fathers, sons and daughters
who face a daily struggle to survive
the bombs, missiles and sniper's bullet,
lack of food, water or medical help -
these human pawns in a game of chance,
played by politicians with no regard,
it would appear, for the sanctity of life.
God of Justice we pray both for victims
and perpetrators that this might end,
along with the fear, hatred and prejudice
that combine to start so many wars.

Bless all those who are,
through no fault of their own,
forced to flee their homes
and take, along with family,
only that which they can carry
and seek a safer place to live.
Remind us of our Saviour who,
as a child, was also a refugee,
finding shelter in a foreign land,
and give us hearts and hands
willing to reach out and help
these, our distant relatives
within your worldwide family.

God of Justice, there is something wrong
when one human being is forced to work
in dangerous and insanitary conditions
for what others consider loose change,
so that another human being can buy,
for next to nothing, a new dress or shirt
that might be worn for one night only
and then replaced by something new.
Forgive us, who have lost our sense of value,
and closed our minds to the truth we know,
that cheap prices often have a hidden cost.

Comfort those
for whom time
has yet to ease
the pain of loss
and emptiness;
broken hearts
that still beat,
but are scarred
by the memory
of a tragic day
that should not
have happened.
Comfort them,
as you have done
and always will,
Gracious God.

(prayer for Aberfan in Wales, and others affected by disasters
caused by human carelessness)

Let your light so shine
within this world
that all lying hidden
within the shadows
might be revealed -
all falsehood, envy,
prejudice and greed -
that which seeks to sow
the seeds of distrust,
suspicion and fear.
Shine brightly, Lord,
within this world,
that those who walk
within the shadows
might step outside
into the warmth
of your light and love.

In a world which cares more
for the needs of self than others,
and is increasingly becoming
more inward-looking and fractured,
give us a heart for the vulnerable,
the refugee, the forgotten, the lost;
a heart that is based on yours,
poured out for the needs of many
and not for the comfort of a few.
Give us a heart which looks out
and sees your beauty in all people,
and welcomes them as a friend.

Be with the victims, Lord,
huddled in basements
and makeshift hospitals,
the grieving, injured,
thirsty, cold and hungry.
Be with the heroes, Lord,
doctors and nurses
in dreadful conditions
putting their lives at risk
so that others might live.
Be with the politicians
in comfortable places,
and the military officers
with the power to stop
this continuing tragedy.
Sow love into the desert
within their hearts, Lord,
and by your Spirit, let it grow.

Bless those who,
at this time of year,
provide shelter
for the homeless,
the refugee,
and those in need;
and in doing so
bring to mind
the charitable act
of a stable owner
in Bethlehem
many years ago.

We pray for families torn apart by explosion
of missile or artillery round,
and those living in fear
of rocket launch or terrorist fire -
wherever they might be,
whoever they might be -
for they are united in their adversity and distress.
Bring comfort, peace and refreshment
for those whose hearts are dry.
We pray for leaders who have no regard
for the sanctity of human life
in pursuit of ideologies or political ambition -
wherever they might be,
whoever they might be -
for they are united in their arrogance and wilfulness.
Bring wisdom, love and repentance
for those whose hearts are cold.
For your love is far greater than the hatred of this world,
far greater than the sorrows of this world.
Infuse this world with your love
and begin with us, we pray.

Loving God we bring to you
those whose hearts and lives
have become distorted,
moulded by the cruel rhetoric
of religious intolerance
into agents of terror,
with no regard
for the sanctity of human life.
Speak into their situation, Lord,
and as the master potter
transform those hearts of stone
into vessels that can be filled,
and even overflow, with love


Help us see this world
through your eyes,
You who saw
what you had made
and were well pleased.

Help us see humanity
through your eyes,
You who saw
we were alone
and gave us family.

Help us see ourselves
through your eyes
You whose love
extends to all,
who died to set us free.

We are moulded, each one of us,
in the image of God,
and within our souls there is a fingerprint
none can erase.
We pray for those who have no regard
for anyone but self,
who put no value on human life.
For nations and individuals who abuse and kill.
We are not called to be judge or jury,
but we are called to be agents of change,
and if the butterfly that flaps its wings
should be our attitude to others
then so be it, Lord,
and may the hurricane this generates
somewhere within the world
reach into the hearts and souls of those
for whom we pray, and reveal to them
how precious are those
for whom they have no love,
and how precious are they
who now bring tears to the eyes of God.

Loving God, we pray
for those whose lives
have been cut short
by acts of violence
fuelled by hatred
or religious zeal,
and the individuals
who perpetrate
such horrific acts.
May those who mourn
for loved ones lost
feel the warmth
of your compassion,
and those who rejoice
at such loss of life
meet face to face
the one true God
and understand
the difference
that love can make.

Grant wisdom to those
who have a heart and vision
for breaking down barriers
that divide communities.
May the seed they scatter
through their words and work
find good soil in which to grow,
and greater understanding
and new friendships be the
harvest that is gathered.

You call us, Lord, to live
lives that are defined
by one word, radical;
to become change-makers
and reformers,
not defined by this world
but by your love and grace,
living as disciples,
proclaiming your word,
making a difference
where we live and work.
But today, Lord, we pray
for all those for whom
to be radicalized
means to take up arms,
subscribe to hate
and follow an altogether
different doctrine...
and the families who fear
a child they love is now sadly lost.
God of mercy, sow seeds of love
within those tangled minds,
that they might hear your voice
and, before it is too late
reach for the hand
held out for them to grasp.

We pray justice
for the falsely accused
freedom for the wrongly imprisoned
healing for the tortured or abused
care for the orphan and widow
concern for the refugee and dispossessed
and above all forgiveness
for our emotional detachment.
May we weep as you weep
love as you love
and not be afraid to be angry
for the sake of your children
wherever they might be.
In our helplessness we ask
Lord, enfold them in your love.

When cries for justice
are met by violence,
tear gas and military response,
and lawlessness
only adds to the suffering
of local communities,
be the peace that speaks
into these situations,
the truth that calls for
repentance,
the love that demands
forgiveness
and the healer
who brings wholeness
into broken lives
and neighbourhoods.

Creator God, we give thanks
that science is continuing
to increase our understanding
of the world we live upon
and the bodies we live within.
We pray that knowledge gained
by research and technology
might not simply be profit-driven,
but kindle a growing desire
for the common good of all,
that rich and poor alike
might see the benefit
and humankind become,
as in the time of Eden,
good stewards of this earth.

As we write a note
or open a book
help us remember
the children for whom
school is aspiration,
the reality, slavery.
As our day begins
may we be thankful
for the little we have,
remembering always
that this is so much more
than millions can only
dare to dream about.

For mothers-to-be
giving birth today
in difficult, remote
and unsanitary conditions
with no midwife's help,
pain relief
or hospital support,
Lord of love and life
we pray for their safety,
freedom from fear,
a safe delivery
and a loving home
for this new arrival
into our beautiful
but often fragile world.


Lord, it is not a just and equal world
when half of this world's wealth
is owned by just one percent
of those who live upon it,
and politicians encourage greed
as "a valuable spur to economic activity."
Where 800 million struggle
each day to find enough to eat
whilst 34000 bank employees
share $12 billion in bonuses.
Lord, you did not create us to be
the selfish people we have become,
but to be stewards of this world
and all that you have given,
to become good neighbours,
compassionate, willing to share.
Forgive us, and give your church
a voice to stand up for those
who are the victims of our greed.

May these feet tread
the road of peace,
these arms share
the hand of peace,
this voice bring
a word of peace,
this life breathe
your peace, shalom,
wherever I might go.

We bring to you, Lord
all those without
adequate provision
of clean water, sanitation,
health care, nutrition,
the right to work
and education,
freedom of thought
and of expression,
freedom from slavery
and discrimination;
all those denied
basic human rights,
but in your eyes
declared equal.
We pray for justice,
equality, compassion
and your will to be done
on earth as it is in heaven.

There is more to peace
than a temporary
cessation of hostility,
political solutions
cannot undo such
wilful disregard
for human life.
First must come
repentance,
forgiveness
and finally, shalom.
God of grace,
work in hearts
torn apart by hate,
pour upon them
your healing balm of love;
bring wholeness,
restoration and hands
that reach out to embrace
rather than cause more pain.
Bring your peace,
your shalom.



Spirit of peace
blow through this world.
Spirit of light
your brightness shown.
Spirit of love
warm hearts grown cold.
Spirit of truth
your word made known.

Bring peace, Lord,
to a world that is troubled;
that peace which transcends
our understanding,
and brings healing
to broken hearts and lives,
that peace which can only come
from the heart of God.

Bless those working
to bring peace
between nations,
cultures and communities;
between families,
neighbours and individuals,
for through peace
comes understanding
and reconciliation,
and within peace
a seed of love is sown
which if nurtured
and encouraged
will, in blossoming
spread its sweet perfume.

Bless the generosity
of the rich and powerful
for the gift of thoughtfulness.

Bless the peacemakers
working in conditions
that are often hazardous.

Bless the politicians
whether good or bad
for decisions affecting all of us.

Bless our words and actions
as we carry your light
into places shrouded in darkness.

Bless your children
whoever they might be
with the warmth of your love and grace.

# 6 : MISSION

Help us to share
the faith we live,
not through force
of argument
or eloquent prose,
but by the blessing
we can bring
into someone's life
through a simple act,
a gentle word,
the gift of peace
or a quiet prayer.

As a heartbeat
carries blood,
newly refreshed
by air we breathe
into every part
of our bodies,
may our lives,
refreshed by prayer
and Holy Spirit,
carry your love
and gift of life
into this world.


You have called us
to make disciples,
but first we must
become disciples,
true followers,
walking together
in your footsteps,
becoming like you
in life and service,
drawing others
who are wandering
into your light.
You have called us
to make disciples.
Enable us, we pray.

God, grant us courage
to speak your name
in conversations
where yesterday
we would have not.
Replace hesitancy
with certainty, we pray.


May your light
so shine within us
and be reflected
through our lives
that we become
your beacons
in this sea of life,
drawing others
away from rocks
and hidden dangers,
showing the way
when the night is dark.


Use us as lamps
within our families,
communities,
places of work,
spheres of influence.
Use us as lamps
to guide the feet
of those who live
unknowingly
within the shadows,
into the warmth
of your light and love.

Bless those whose mission field
is parents and young children;
providing a welcoming space,
fellowship where they can feel safe,
activities for letting off steam,
a chance to talk and share concerns,
precious time to simply unwind.
And in the midst, your love revealed
in open hearts and helping hands
reaching out into the community.
Bless them, and the parents, guardians
and children as they meet together,
that through this work, seeds of love
might be sown and, in due time, blossom..

Spirit of peace
blow through this world.
Spirit of light
your brightness shown.
Spirit of love
warm hearts grown cold.
Spirit of truth
your word made known.

# 7 : SIGNS OF HOPE

Yours is the love
that in a moment of divine joy
announced, "Let there be light!"
and in a blaze of glory
revealed the master plan
of a garden we now walk upon.
Creative love,
Enduring love,
Patient love,
Forgiving love,
Yours is the love
that in such suffering and pain
announced, "The price is paid!"
and in a blaze of glory
revealed the Master's plan
of Salvation that we depend upon.
Yours is the love!

Bless those who, with a word
or hug, can bring a smile
onto the face of someone
who is struggling with life -
a simple, inexpensive
but infinitely precious gift
from one heart to another.


Jesus Christ, Good Shepherd,
loving and embracing
the vulnerable and weak,
looking for the fallen,
searching for the lost,
be with all who work
with those whose lives
have been devastated by loss,
whether by natural disaster
or human fault.
Grant them courage,
strength and protection,
these loving shepherds,
who willingly choose
to place their own lives at risk
in often dangerous situations
that others might now live.

Bless those whose faith,
even when tested
by pain, loss or sorrow,
still shines through
the darkness of their lives
as a witness to you,
and speaks so clearly
of your love for them.
Bless them, for their witness
to your grace and mercy,
and hold them gently
in the comfort of your arms.


For small miracles
in the midst of tragedy
we thank you, Lord.
For refugees rescued
from sinking ships,
earthquake victims
brought alive from
upturned buildings,
and the many others
that go unnoticed
in our daily lives,
where acts of love
and selfless bravery
confront misfortune
and catastrophe
and from the darkness
bring light and life.

For the courage of relief workers
operating in desperate conditions
bring a blessing to their lives.
For the generosity of ordinary people
giving to those who have lost so much
bring a blessing to their lives.
For selfless love wherever it is shown
which gives without considering cost
bring a blessing to their lives.

We give thanks for generosity!
For billionaires giving of their wealth
to establish research programs
for the eradication of disease;
volunteers giving of their time
to help those less fortunate
in their neighbourhood, city
or in some remote disaster zone;
and of course the widow's mite,
given without counting cost
and no less generous a gift.
For all such generosity,
which comes from one heart
and flows freely to another,
as does your love for us,
we thank you, generous God!

May lives be blessed, Lord,
wherever generosity is shown.
The giving of time to help
when someone is in need.
The always-being-there
as children finally leave home.
That spontaneous purchase
as a token of someone's love.
The sharing of resources
with those who do not have.
The freewill offering
for the ministry of your Church,
and the digging deep
for a charitable cause.
Wherever generosity is shown,
may lives be blessed, dear Lord.


Breathe love into lives ruled by fear
Soften hearts that are hardened by pride
Whisper gently to those bound by chains
Sow peace where conflict divides

# 7 : BLESSINGS

May God's Word be in your heart.
May God's Word be on your lips.
May God's Word be in your touch.
May God's Word direct your feet.
On this day and all your days to come
May God's Word be the life you live.


Be a blessing to us, O God,
as we enter this new day;
our guide along the road,
a hand to hold,
an encouraging word,
the air we breathe,
our joy of life.
As we enter this new day,
be a blessing to us, O God.

May the blessing of love be ours
May the blessing of joy be ours
May the blessing of peace be ours
May the blessing of patience be ours
May the blessing of kindness be ours
May the blessing of generosity be ours
May the blessing of faithfulness be ours
May the blessing of gentleness be ours
May the blessing of self-control be ours
That we might become a blessing
to others through your Holy Spirit
flowing freely from our hearts.

May God bless
every step we take,
every word we speak,
every hand we shake,
every truth we seek,
every prayer we make.
May God bless
this day and all days
our departing,
our travelling
and our returning.
God bless
our minds
our hearts
our faith.
God bless
our words
our hands
our feet.

The grace of God the Father
be the motivation
for all that we do and say.
The love of God the Son
be the inspiration
for the many words we pray.
The power of God the Spirit
be in the expression
of a living faith this day.

May the blessings of the earth surround you.
Clear paths and firm ground to walk upon,
fresh water and green shoots to sustain you.
May the blessings of the sky surround you.
Rising sun to lighten your journey,
soft rain in due season to refresh you.
May the blessings of heaven surround you.
Angel voices to raise your spirits,
the Father's arms to lift and embrace you.

God's love direct your actions,
God's truth be in your words,
God's joy infuse your spirit,
God's peace be in your hearts.

God bless you in rising,
through dawn chorus
and cheerfulness.
God bless you in working,
through honest toil
and service.
God bless you in sharing,
through spoken word
and embracing.
God bless you in resting,
through peaceful sleep
and protection.

May the peace of God
be your companion
wherever you may walk,
a constant strength,
a helping hand,
and tireless friend.

Bless, Lord, the words I speak
that they might bring comfort.
Bless, Lord, these hands I use
that they might be of service.
Bless, Lord, this path I tread
that it might be safe to travel.
Bless, Lord, this life I live
that it might bring you glory.

May the love of Jesus Christ
bring us wholeness,
the  grace of God the Father
grant us peace,
the breath of Holy Spirit
instil passion
and the unity between them
give us strength
for this and every day.

May the Father's hand
keep you from stumbling,
the footprints of Jesus
give you confidence to follow,
and the fire of the Spirit
keep you warm and safe
in your walk with God this day.

May the love of God
be the ocean that you sail on
and the grace of God
bring you calm in stormy days.
May the word of God
guide you to your destination
and the breath of God
speed you safely on your way.

The blessing of the God of life be with us
in our journeying
The blessing of the risen Christ be with us
in our following
The blessing of the Holy Spirit be with us
in our questioning
The blessing of the heavenly host be with us
in our worshipping
Bless, O God, each hour, each day,
that we shall walk with you.

May the cleansing water
of God's love refresh you,
the gentle breeze
of God's Spirit revive you,
and the radiance
of God's Son surround you,
this day and all days. Amen
God's presence be with you,
Spirit's breath refresh you,
Son's love sustain you
and the power of the Three
be revealed through your life
today and every day. Amen.

May God be with you
through the storms of life,
a safe haven,
voice of calm,
reassurance,
healing balm,
and when storms are over
bring you safely home.


A song of joy be in your heart
At the beginning of the day,
And at work and relaxation
God beside to guide the way;
And when the day is closing
And the moon shares its soft light
May your soul be filled with peace
Within the stillness of the night.


This day, and all days, having rested
safely within the Father's warmth,
may you be refreshed by Spirit's breath,
nourished by living water and bread,
and know the fellowship of God
beside you, wherever you may be led.

John Birch

# ABOUT THE AUTHOR

John Birch is a Methodist lay preacher and writer living in South Wales, and has a website www.faithandworship.com which is a well-used resource of prayer and Bible study material Also available in paperback and Kindle is *The Act of Prayer*, a collection of 700 lectionary-themed prayers.

John Birch

Made in the USA
San Bernardino, CA
14 May 2017